W9-CJD-907

LIFE DURING THE

GREAT CIVILIZATIONS

The Vikings

LIFE DURING THE GREAT CIVILIZATIONS

The Vikings

Don Nardo

BLACKBIRCH PRESS

An imprint of Thomson Gale, a part of The Thomson Corporation

Detroit • New York • San Francisco • San Diego • New Haven, Conn. • Waterville, Maine • London • Munich

For more information, contact
Blackbirch Press
27500 Drake Rd.
Farmington Hills, MI 48331-3535
Or you can visit our Internet site at http://www.gale.com

Photo credits: See page 48.

LIBRARY OF CONGRESS CATALOGING-IN-PUBLICATION DATA

Nardo, Don, 1947-

The Vikings / by Don Nardo.
    p. cm. — (Life during the great civilizations)
Includes bibliographical references and index.
ISBN 1-4103-0584-8 (hard cover : alk. paper)
1. Vikings—Juvenile literature. 2. Northmen—Juvenile literature. I. Title. II. Series.

DL65.N27 2005
948'.022—dc22
                                                    2005007025

Printed in United States
10 9 8 7 6 5 4 3 2 1

Contents

Raiders and Explorers in a Violent Age

"**F**rom the fury of the Northmen, deliver us, O Lord!"[1] This was a common prayer spoken across large sections of northern Europe in medieval times. Today, the fearsome characters mentioned in the prayer—the Northmen—are better known as the Vikings. From roughly A.D. 790 to 1100, they raided farms, churches, villages, and towns far and wide. For this reason, modern historians often call this violent period the Viking Age.

During these years, the people of England, Ireland, France, and other nearby lands lived in fear of the sight of approaching Viking "dragon ships" so called because their prows often featured wooden carvings of dragons' heads. Armed with large metal swords and battle-axes, Viking raiders often seemed to appear out of nowhere. They looted, burned, raped, and killed at will. At first, they attacked only coastal areas. But as time went on, they grew bolder, sailed down rivers, and assaulted towns lying far inland. In March 845, for instance, a large force of Vikings moved down the Seine River and laid siege to Paris.

The Vikings were the early medieval inhabitants of what are now Denmark, Norway, and Sweden. This is why they were sometimes called Danes, Norsemen, and Swedes, as

Opposite Page: The terrified inhabitants of an English town prepare to face the fury of a Viking raid.

7

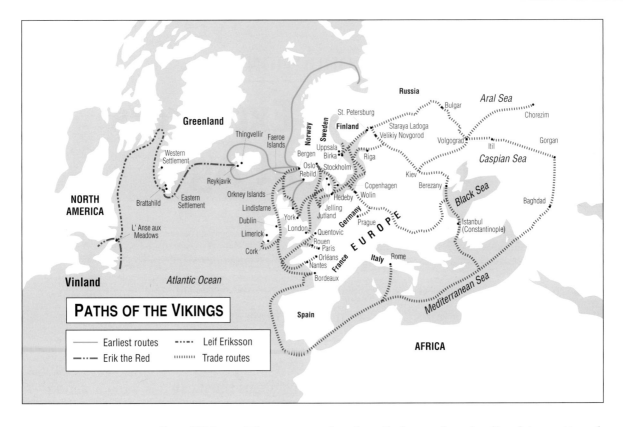

PATHS OF THE VIKINGS

Earliest routes — Leif Eriksson
Erik the Red ...... Trade routes

well as Vikings. They were a hardy tribal people who lived in scattered villages and small kingdoms located mostly along the rugged Scandinavian coasts. Usually the Viking tribes and kingdoms operated independently. Each had its own leaders and looked after its own interests. On occasion several smaller Viking groups might band together, but there was no overall Viking nation.

Although the Viking raiders from these groups rightfully earned a nasty reputation as raiders and killers, not all Vikings took part in the raids. Raiding was only one way the Viking peoples made a living. In fact, most Vikings were farmers, craftsmen, and traders. They were also highly skilled sailors and explorers. Viking groups founded settlements in Ireland, Iceland, and Greenland in the west. They even reached and briefly colonized the shores of North America, probably

The Lindisfarne Raid

The first major Viking raid into Christian Europe occurred in June 793. The target was the tiny island of Lindisfarne, off the eastern coast of Britain. Swarming ashore, the Viking warriors looted and burned the Christian monastery that dominated the island. A horrified Christian scholar of that period wrote:

> Never before has such terror appeared in Britain, as we have now suffered from a pagan race. Nor was it thought possible that such an inroad from the sea could be made. Behold the Church of St. Cuthbert, spattered with the blood of the priests of God, despoiled of all its ornaments. A place more venerable [dignified and respected] than any other in Britain has fallen prey to pagans.

Parts of the monastery at Lindisfarne still survive intact.

around the year 1000. In the east, they settled in Russia and traded with peoples as far south as Arabia.

In most cases, once they settled down somewhere, the Vikings quickly adopted the local customs, including language and religious beliefs. As a result, the old Viking culture steadily disappeared. The major exception was Iceland, where a number of Viking customs survived longer. But in most parts of Europe, the once fearsome Vikings had faded into the realm of legend by the thirteenth century.

CHAPTER ONE

Viking Homes and Families

Though Viking raids were common in early medieval Europe, warfare was only one facet of Viking culture. After military campaigns were over, the fighters returned to peaceful, productive villages and towns. There, the warriors were greeted by their families, as well as by farmers, craftsmen, and merchants who rarely or never went to war. Their houses were usually large and well built. And their occupations, family life, and social customs were diverse and in many ways sophisticated.

These average Vikings worked to create comfortable, safe, and happy home lives. The proof for this comes partly from surviving examples of Viking poetry. A verse from one of a group of writings known as the *Rune Poems* translates roughly: "Bliss he enjoys who knows not suffering, sorrow nor anxiety, and has prosperity and happiness and a good enough house."[2]

Other evidence for the Viking quest for domestic comfort, security, and prosperity comes from modern excavations of Viking villages and houses. For example, most towns had streets made of wooden planks laid out in long rows. Narrower wooden walkways connected individual houses to the streets. These wooden streets and walkways made getting around town easier and kept people from dirtying their feet in the mud. Towns also typically had outer defenses made of big mounds of earth and wooden palisades. These kept the inhabitants safe from raiders. Towns also had craft shops, blacksmith forges, shipyards, barns for food storage, and other facilities to support the community and its inhabitants.

Sturdy Houses

The houses in such towns were practical and sometimes large and comfortable. From a construction standpoint, there was no typical Viking house. Building materials varied according to the region and what was readily available there. Hardwood forests covered much of medieval Denmark, for instance. So, many of the Viking houses in that area were built from hardwood posts and planks. Farther north, in

Norway, log cabins similar to those in the early American frontier were common. In contrast, Iceland had few forests. So the Vikings who lived there built their homes with field stones and mounds of earth.

Still another variation was wattle-and-daub construction. This was particularly common in poor farmhouses located away from the larger towns. Builders dug a pit and erected the house's walls around the edges. The walls consisted of wattle or interwoven tree branches, smeared with daub (clay, plaster, or dung). The ceiling was made of thickly interwoven branches and straw, called thatch.

Whatever the materials used, a majority of houses throughout the Viking lands had a similar layout. They had a large central hall, or living room. In the middle was a big hearth made of field stones, which provided warmth and cooking facilities. The smoke from the fire exited through a hole in the ceiling. Some homes also had small clay ovens on or beside the hearth for baking bread.

Around the edges of the central hall ran a low wooden or earthen platform. On this the family members laid wool blankets and/or pillows

stuffed with chicken or duck feathers. This is where most Vikings slept. Only the residents of the richest homes could afford real beds. Such beds closely resembled modern wood-frame versions and had mattresses stuffed with bird feathers. Richer homes also sometimes had two or three smaller rooms leading off the main one. These might be bed chambers or workrooms for spinning, weaving, or tanning hides, for example.

Other than pillows and mattresses, Viking homes had few luxuries. There were usually no windows, so as to keep heat from escaping. And there were no inside bathrooms. People used small wooden outhouses located beside or in back of their houses. The toilet was a simple latrine, a hole dug in the ground.

Close-Knit Families

The families who lived in these houses were close-knit. In fact, the loyalty and teamwork of family members resembled that seen among Viking warriors in battle. A typical family consisted of a father, mother, and children. Grandparents, widowed aunts, and one or two slaves might also live in a Viking home. Slaves, called thralls, were foreigners who were either captured in war or bought in slave markets.

All members of a family, including the slaves, if any, worked hard to support the family. Fathers and grown sons raised crops and livestock or engaged in craftwork. Typical crafts included tanning; metalworking, including making swords, axes, and jewelry; woodworking; and shipbuilding. Other men were merchants who traded locally-made

Actresses at a museum portray Viking women making clothes and preparing food.

products for items made in distant towns. Some men also took part in the infamous Viking raids, which often brought home valuable supplies of gold, livestock, and slaves.

Adult men usually ran Viking households. However, when warriors were away on campaigns, their wives or mothers took complete control of the family. Viking women were often as independent, tough, and capable as the men. A mother raised her children, cooked, and made the family's clothes. She also taught her daughters how to perform these duties, since there were no formal schools. A woman could divorce an abusive husband by making a formal complaint to adult witnesses. And some women took up weapons and fought alongside their fathers, husbands, and sons when their village came under attack.

Good and Plentiful Food

The food grown or raised by the men and prepared and cooked by the women was both varied and hearty. Bread, made from barley or other grains, was a staple. A verse from a Viking poem, the *Rigspula*, mentions such bread, along with other appetizing items in a big family feast:

> Then took Mother a figured cloth, white, of linen, and covered the board [table]; thereafter took she a fine-baked loaf, white of wheat and covered the cloth. Next she brought forth plenteous dishes . . . and spread the board with brown-fried bacon and roasted birds. There was wine in a vessel and rich-wrought goblets.[3]

The roasted birds were likely ducks or chickens. And the bacon came from pigs, a common farm animal in the Viking lands. Other meats the Vikings enjoyed included lamb, beef, goat, deer, elk, rabbit, bear, seal, and whale.

Viking families also consumed large amounts of fruits and vegetables. The vegetables were often combined with hunks of meat in piping hot stews. The most common vegetables were cabbage, peas, race of murderous giants, enemies of the gods, often tried to cross the bridge. But they were prevented from doing so by the mighty guardian god Heimdall.

Within Asgard were many estates, each the home of a major god. The chief god, Odin, had the largest estate and castle. Also on his lands was Valhalla (the "Hall of the Heroes"), the place where the souls of Viking warriors went. After these heroes fell in battle, a group of divine women warriors—the Valkyries, or Mead-Maidens—took them to Valhalla. Other important gods who lived in Asgard and interacted with the souls of dead Vikings were Thor and Freya. Thor was the master of weather, wind, thunder, and lightning. Freya, Odin's daughter, was the goddess of love and fertility.

The Valkyries lead dead Viking warriors to Valhalla in this modern painting.

Viking Funerals and Burials

In the year 922, a Muslim traveler named Ibn Fadlan witnessed the funeral of a Viking chief on the shores of the Baltic Sea. Fadlan said that the dead man's body was placed on a raised platform on a Viking ship. Beside the body lay that of a slave girl who was killed so that she could serve her master in the afterlife. Dead animals and other foodstuffs, as well as weapons, were also placed in the boat. Then the chief's relatives and friends set the boat on fire and watched it burn.

A dead Viking warrior receives a fiery send-off.

Archaeologists have confirmed that well-to-do Vikings did have such elaborate funerals. Sometimes the vessels were buried in the earth rather than burned. The remains of one such funeral boat were uncovered in 1903 in Oseberg, Norway. Ordinary Vikings were buried inside mounds of earth or underground chambers. They, too, were surrounded with weapons, clothes, food, and other items intended for use in the afterlife.

The Vikings believed that these gods, aided by dead human heroes, held back the forces of evil and chaos. According to pagan Viking religious beliefs, the future was hopeless and bleak. And eventually, they thought, a huge battle would take place. In this conflict, known as Ragnarok (the "Twilight of the Gods"), the gods and heroes would fight the evil forces. And the gods and men would lose. Both the gods and humanity would be destroyed. But despite the knowledge that they were doomed, these good races would continue to struggle to the bitter end. "Heaven is cloven [cut in half]," the *Elder Edda* says of Ragnarok. "The sun turns black, earth sinks into the sea, [and] the hot stars down from heaven are whirled. . . . [This is] the fate of the gods, the mighty in [the] fight [to end all fights]."[5]

The Coming of Christianity

The hopelessness of this view of divine and human fate contrasted sharply with the Christian beliefs the Vikings eventually adopted. According to Christian tradition, after death the souls of the faithful will enjoy eternal bliss in heaven. Many Vikings found this concept

In this painting, the Earth sinks into the sea in the climax of Ragnarok, the Twilight of the Gods.

hopeful and compelling. Most of Denmark, as well as Iceland, had converted to the new faith by the year 1000. By 1050, the Vikings in Norway had followed suit. And the Swedish Vikings were all Christians by the late 1100s.

These transitions from pagan to Christian beliefs and practices were not sudden. At first, a number of Vikings held on to some of the old ways even after they had accepted Jesus Christ. This can be seen in the kinds of tokens people wore. It was common practice, for example, to wear a Christian cross that also represented Thor's famous

This reconstructed Viking church is typical of the many Christian churches the Vikings erected.

Built in 1150, the Viking stave church at Borgund, Norway, survives almost completely intact.

weapon, the hammer. In addition, for at least a generation or two, some Vikings conducted pagan sacrifices in secret one day and then attended their local Christian churches the next.

The Christian churches that sprang up around the Viking world were the most obvious outward sign of the new faith. The first Viking churches were one-story wooden structures that resembled typical houses. But by the early 1200s, huge, multistoried churches began to emerge.

Churches replaced forests as the centers of religious worship in the Viking world. Priests rang their church bells to summon the faithful to services and also, people believed, to ward off any of the old gods who might try to intrude. Inside the church, new members of the congregation underwent the rite of baptism. As happens in many modern churches, a priest dipped part of the person's body in holy water. The baptized person then wore white clothes for a week following the ceremony.

Another common practice of Viking Christians was to build reliquaries. These were decorated wooden boxes in which people stored holy relics. Such artifacts included crosses, pieces of clothing, or even bones belonging to respected religious leaders and saints. The lingering influence of older Viking ways can be seen in the carved dragons' heads that decorated many of the reliquaries. This and other evidence shows that, both before and after the coming of Christianity, the Vikings were a spiritual and god-fearing people.

CHAPTER THREE

Leisure Activities and Sports

In the midst of busy lives filled with work, family duties, chores, and warfare, the Vikings found time for fun and leisure activities. In fact, evidence shows that they played every bit as hard as they fought in battle. Among the many leisure pastimes enjoyed in the Viking lands were outdoor sports. Especially popular were those that stressed strength and endurance or rough contact with one's opponents. But the Vikings liked tamer, indoor leisure activities, too—ones in which all family members could participate.

Indoor Fun

One very popular indoor activity was playing board games. The Vikings played a checkerslike game known as Morels. It used playing pieces made of glass or polished stones. Another popular board game was Hnefatafl, meaning "King's Table." Evidence shows that it was played in parts of Scandinavia as early as A.D. 400. The rules of the game have been lost, but modern scholars believe it was similar in some ways to chess. Chess steadily replaced Hnefatafl in late medieval times, although the older game was still played in Wales as late as 1587.

Of the indoor, family-oriented Viking pastimes, the most popular was partying and feasting. It was common for one family to invite several other families over to enjoy a huge spread of food. The biggest feast day in the Viking world was Yule. Held on January 12, it celebrated the turn of the season, the moment when the shorter days of winter began to grow longer. On such occasions, women prepared dozens of tasty dishes.

The entertainment during such get-togethers was diverse. Sometimes young boys put on a show of mock fighting for the adults. Viking boys often played with wooden swords and shields. Their mock battles were a form of play. But they had a serious dimension, too, because the fighting skills learned this way were often used later in real battles.

After cheering on the boy fighters, the partygoers might call for a storyteller to step forward. In an age without radio, television, and movies, storytelling was a favorite pastime. Some people who had acting talent and good speaking voices became skilled at reciting famous tales of Viking gods and human heroes. The most skilled storytellers— the skalds—were in great demand. They often traveled from one town to another and actually made a living by telling stories. In contrast, the least skilled storytellers were called jesters. They were sometimes booed and scorned when they did not please a crowd.

At right shows
actual game
tokens used by
Vikings. The inset
is a modern
reconstruction of
a Hnefatafl board.

Music and Singing

Evidence suggests that the skalds and other storytellers enlivened their tales with songs. Thus, the best skalds were also skilled singers and musicians. Almost all Vikings loved music and enjoyed singing. It was not unusual for men to sing while rowing their ships or working in the fields or on the docks. People sang drinking songs at parties. And parents sang lullabies to their small children.

Singing was so popular that it mattered little whether one had a pleasant singing voice, at least to the Vikings. Foreigners who heard the Vikings sing often had a different opinion, however. An Arab merchant who visited Denmark in the tenth century later wrote: "Never before have I heard uglier songs than those of the Vikings. . . . The growling sound coming from their throats reminds me of dogs howling, only more untamed."[6]

In fairness to the Vikings, the man who wrote these words probably did not hear the best singers and songs in the region. Today it is almost impossible to reconstruct the sounds of that music. This is because the Vikings had no system of music notation. Songs were played and sung from memory, and over time most were forgotten. One possible exception is a song that was written down in Denmark in the fourteenth century, shortly after the introduction of a primitive form of musical notation. Titled "I Dreamed a Dream," it may have been an old Viking song that survived beyond the Viking Age.

One aspect of Viking music that modern scholars know more about is the kinds of instruments the skalds and other musicians played. One, the pan flute, was made from a cow's horn or bone. There were wooden flutes, too, with holes drilled in their sides. Also common was the lur, a long cone-shaped instrument that a person blew into. In addition, the Vikings had stringed instruments, including the rebec, which resembled a violin, and small harps.

Outdoor Sports

In addition to feasting, storytelling, and singing, the Vikings enjoyed more physical outdoor activities, many of them related to fighting and warfare. Viking warriors had to become skilled archers, for example. And archery tournaments were held each year in every town and kingdom. Spear-throwing contests were also popular.

Other popular competitive sports included long-distance swimming and ball playing. In the first, men swam out into the sea until they were afraid to go any farther. The last person to turn back was the winner. The most popular ball game was called knattleikr. Most of its

The Archer and the Apple

A famous story about an expert Viking bowman named Palnatoke and an archery tournament has survived. It dates from the tenth century, but a version of it later became popular in Europe—the story of William Tell, who was compelled to shoot an apple off his young son's head. According to the original Viking version:

William Tell prepares to shoot the apple off his son's head.

[A local king] ordered Palnatoke to shoot an apple off of his own son's head. He would only get one try. Palnatoke had to obey the king's wishes but when the king asked Palnatoke, after he had successfully shot the apple, why he had taken out three arrows before he shot, he replied: "The other two were to avenge my son against you in case I missed with the first."

rules have been lost. It is known that it was a team sport that included some elements of modern baseball, such as hitting a hard ball with a bat, and football, such as tackling the person who caught the ball. Games sometimes went on for days or even weeks.

By far the most popular sport in the Viking world was wrestling. There were three styles, each with its own moves and rules. The first, freestyle wrestling, featured throws, armlocks, headlocks, tackles, and many other moves common in modern wrestling. A second form of Viking wrestling—Glima—was more like modern judo. Opponents wore big belts. Each grasped the other's belt and tried to throw him off balance. (Glima survived in Iceland and remains widely popular there.) Finally, there was "crude wrestling," which allowed tripping, choking, and other "dirty" fighting.

Thus, from tamer activities such as singing and storytelling to rough-and-tough sports like wrestling, there was a leisure pastime to please Vikings of all ages and tastes.

CHAPTER FOUR

Viking Longships and Naval Warfare

The Vikings did not have any advanced technology in the modern sense. They had no electricity, advanced plumbing or heating facilites, or complex machines. However, they did excel at building wooden ships. In fact, during early medieval times, Viking seagoing vessels were more sophisticated than those of any other European people. This is the main reason why the Vikings were so formidable in the areas of trade, exploration, and especially war.

Kinds and Capabilities of Warships

Viking war vessels, renowned for their fine construction and speed, were widely feared. The general Norse name for such ships was langskip, usually translated as "longship." There were several varieties, most often classified by the number of benches, or rowing places (sessa), on a side. One of the smaller warships was a 13-bencher, meaning that it had 13 sessa on each side, for a total of 26 oars. It was called a threttensessa. Ships with roughly 20 to 28 benches (40–56 oars) were known as snekkja. And those with even more benches and oars were called skei or drekar ("dragons"). In 1062 a Viking leader named Harold Hardrada built one of the biggest longships ever, a 35-bencher (with 70 rowers) named the *Great Dragon*.

All Viking longships had similar colorful names. The names were chosen to emphasize the power of these boats, so they often invoked dragons and other mythical creatures as well as powerful animals. Other examples included the *Long Serpent*, *Surf Dragon*, *Oar Steed*, and *Fjord Elk*.

Archaeologists have determined the exact size of many of these ships by studying their remains. In 1962 excavators found five longships at the bottom of a fjord in Denmark. They were 12-benchers, so each originally had 24 rowers. One ship measured 57 feet (17.4m) long by 8.5 feet (2.6m) wide. Each ship was only a few feet deep from top to bottom. Making these ships both narrow and shallow allowed them to sail down shallow rivers and to run up easily onto beaches during raids.

Longships had both oars and sails. The oars were used mainly in coastal waters. When possible, Viking ship captains kept their vessels within sight of land by day and camped on beaches at night. The sails, which were made of linen or wool, were used mostly out in the open ocean. Navigation there was done by watching the stars. Under sail, large longships could reach speeds of up to 20 knots (23 miles per hour).

A Viking ship departs Norway on an expedition. Though small, these vessels were very sturdy.

Building a Longship

Constructing a longship required the skills and labor of dozens of ship-wrights, carpenters, and other experts. The main material of the hull

The Mast and Sail

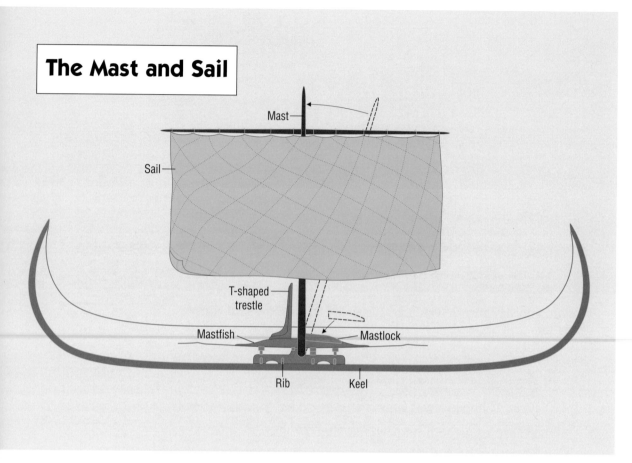

Mast

Sail

T-shaped trestle

Mastfish

Mastlock

Rib

Keel

was oak, chosen for its hardness and durability. Individual elements, such as deck planks and carved animals on the prow and stern, were sometimes made of lighter woods like pine. The principal tools employed were metal axes and saws and iron-headed hammers. Also used were wooden mallets, hand drills for boring holes, and sharp knives and chisels for carving.

The first step in building a longship was to lay out the keel, the central spine running lengthwise along the bottom of the hull. Curved wooden ribs sloped upward from and at right angles to the keel. The hull boards attached to these ribs were called strakes. Each overlapped the one below it, a technique known as clinkering. (Such a vessel is said to be "clinker-built.") The cracks between the strakes were filled and water-sealed with wool that had been soaked in tar.

The main elements of the deck area were the wooden benches for the rowers, the deck boards, and the mast. The benches ran along the vessel's inner sides. The deck planks were often laid down by hand and left loose. That way the crewmen could easily lift them up if they

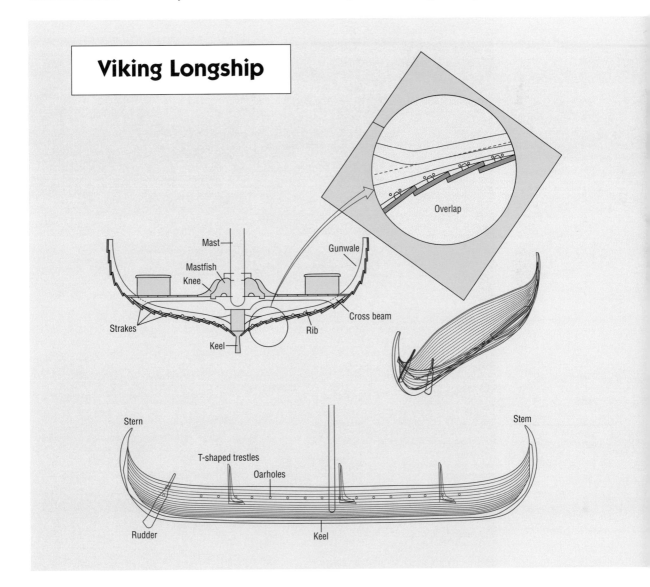

Viking Longship

Overlap

Mast

Mastfish

Knee

Gunwale

Strakes

Cross beam

Rib

Keel

Stern

Stem

T-shaped trestles

Oarholes

Rudder

Keel

Viking warriors
come ashore on
the coast of
France. In this
case, the ships
were used as
troop transports.

wanted to load or unload supplies from the hold below. The bottom section of the mast rested inside a huge block of wood known as the mastfish. A series of ropes connected the mast and sail to the ship's front, back, and sides.

Longships in Battle

One way that Viking longships were used in warfare was to ferry troops to a specific location. The soldiers then went ashore and conducted their land battle or raid. When they were finished, they climbed back aboard the vessels and sailed home.

Warships often saw service in fearsome sea battles, too. The Vikings specialized in hand-to-hand fighting with swords, axes, and spears. So they preferred to make their sea battles as much like land battles as possible. The effect was most striking when two Viking groups fought each other. Each opposing force customarily lashed many of its ships together, creating a large floating platform. The biggest ship, which usually belonged to the commander, was almost always in the middle.

The object was to board the opposing platform and kill as many enemy troops as possible. Boarding was not an easy task, though, because the defenders went to great lengths to protect the platform. First, they sometimes fastened iron plates to the hulls of the ships lining the outside sections of the platform. These kept the enemy from poking hules in the vessels' hulls. Another defensive tactic involved placing iron spikes so that they jutted outward from key positions on the platform. Any enemy ships that strayed too close to the deadly spikes got their hulls pierced and sank.

The attackers tried to get around and through these defenses by using some formidable tactics of their own. As individual longships moved toward the enemy platform, the crews unleashed arrows, spears, and stones. The main purpose of this barrage was to force the defenders back from the outer edges of the platform so the attackers could board more easily. Attempting to survive this lethal barrage, the defenders hid behind their raised shields or wooden barricades set up on deck.

Meanwhile, some men from attacking ships dove into the water. They swam over to the platform and climbed up its sides. Using axes and hammers, some tried to break off any protruding iron spikes so that it would be safer for their ships to approach the platform. Others jumped up onto the platform and tried to establish a position to assault the defenders.

Once the attackers got a strong foothold on the platform, they formed a line and raised their shields. This barrier was designed to

In addition to fierce sea battles, the Vikings fought on land, as in this modern reconstruction of a large-scale coastal raid.

A King Dies in Battle

The sea battle at Svölder occurred around the year 1000. Norway's King Olaf Tryggvasson, with a hundred ships, opposed a larger allied fleet of Danes and Swedes. The heroics of King Olaf's chief archer, Einar Tambarskelve, and Olaf's death in the battle are captured in these excerpts from the *Saga of King Olaf Tryggvasson*:

> Einar Tambarskelve, one of the sharpest of archers, stood by the mast, shooting his bow. He shot an arrow at Earl Eric, which hit the tiller-end above his head so hard that it penetrated up to its shaft. . . . "What was that which broke with such a noise?" called King Olaf. "Norway, king," cried Einar, "[which is slipping] from your grip." . . . The battle was still raging in the forehold, but . . . the earl's men had set out their ship's boats all around the *Serpent* [Olaf's ship] and were killing those who leaped overboard. These men tried to seize the king . . . but [he] threw his shield above his head and sank beneath the surface.

Viking longships navigate rough waters. For several centuries these vessels made the Vikings masters of the sea.

repel the first shower of arrows and stones launched by the defenders. Then the attackers broke their line. Individual warriors rushed forward, swinging their axes and swords and screaming loudly to try to frighten their opponents.

Sometimes such attacks were not successful. The defenders managed to push the attackers back and off the platform. When an attack was successful, the victors cut the enemy ships loose and either kept or sank them.

The drama and sweep of such a battle is illustrated in a surviving Viking writing called the *Saga of King Olaf Tryggvasson*. The following excerpt describes part of the Battle of Svölder, which took place about the year 1000:

> Earl Eric was in the forehold of his ship, where a shield-wall had been set up. Hewing [cutting] weapons—the sword and axe—and thrusting spears alike were being used in the fighting. . . . So many weapons rained down on the *Serpent* . . . that the shields could scarcely withstand them.[7]

Those who survived such battles returned home, some wounded, some not. They were proud of their military exploits and hoped that future generations would remember them and retell their stories. Thanks to the survival of a handful of Viking writings, that wish was fulfilled.

Notes

Introduction: Raiders and Explorers in a Violent Age

1. Quoted in Howard La Fay, *The Vikings*. Washington, DC: National Geographic, 1972, p. 8.

Chapter 1: Viking Homes and Families

2. Quoted in Bruce Dickins, ed., *Runic and Heroic Poems*. 1915. Reprint: Whitefish, MT: Kessinger, 2003, p. 12.
3. *Rigspula*, in Olive Bray, ed. and trans., *The Elder or Poetic Edda*. New York: AMS, 1908, p. 108.
4. Quoted in Dickins, *Runic and Heroic Poems*, p. 13.

Chapter 2: Religious Beliefs and Practices

5. Quoted in Mircea Eliade, ed., *Essential Sacred Writings from Around the World*. San Francisco: HarperCollins, 1967, p. 125.

Chapter 3: Leisure Activities and Sports

6. Quoted in Mogens Friis, "Vikings and Their Music," April 15, 2000. www.viking.no/e/life/music/e-musikk-mogens.html.

Chapter 4: Viking Longships and Naval Warfare

7. Quoted in Ian Heath, *The Vikings*. Oxford, England: Osprey, 2001, p. 57.

Glossary

amulets: Objects, either worn or carried, that were believed to have magical properties.

Glima: A form of Viking wrestling that resembled modern judo.

Hnefatafl: A medieval board game similar to chess.

knattleikr: A Viking ball game that may have featured elements of both baseball and football.

lur: A long, cone-shaped musical instrument used in medieval Scandinavia.

palisades: Tall fences used for defensive purposes.

rebec: A medieval stringed instrument similar to a violin.

reliquaries: Boxes for storing sacred objects.

sanctuaries: Areas where religious worship takes place.

sessa: Benches on which the rowers on Viking ships sat.

skalds: Viking storytellers and singers.

skei: A large Viking warship.

strakes: Hull boards on a Viking ship.

thralls: Viking slaves.

For More Information

Books

Melvin Berger, *The Real Vikings: Craftsmen, Traders, and Fearsome Raiders*. Washington, DC: National Geographic, 2003.

Peter Hicks, *Technology in the Time of the Vikings*. Austin, TX: Raintree Steck-Vaughn, 1998.

Joann Jovinelly, *The Crafts and Culture of the Vikings*. New York: Rosen, 2002.

Angus Konstam, *Historical Atlas of the Viking World*. New York: Checkmark, 2002.

Hazel Martell, *Food and Feasts with the Vikings*. Morristown, NJ: New Discovery, 1995.

———, *What Do We Know About the Vikings?* New York: Peter Bedrick, 1992.

Web Sites

Explore a Viking Village (www.pbs.org/wgbh/nova/vikings/village.html). An excellent site containing several videos, each of which takes the viewer on a journey through a separate part of a Viking village.

Rigspula (www.gale.pwp.blueyonder.co.uk/midnite_gale_13.htm). Contains Olive Bray's excellent English translation of one of the major poems collected in the Icelandic Viking *Elder Edda*.

The Viking Network (www.viking.no/e/index.html). This site has many links that lead to short, readable articles about many different aspects of Viking life.

Index

Picture Credits

About the Author

Historian Don Nardo has published many volumes for young readers about ancient and medieval civilizations, including *The Roman Empire, A Travel Guide to Ancient Alexandria, The Etruscans, Empires of Mesopotamia, The Byzantine Empire, Life on a Medieval Pilgrimage,* and *Weapons and Warfare of the Middle Ages.* He lives in Massachusetts with his wife, Christine.

HOAKX +
948
.022
N

NARDO, DON
    THE VIKINGS

OAK FOREST
12/05